KNOW YOUR BIRD SOUNDS

Volume 1: Songs and Calls of
Yard, Garden, and City Birds

KNOW YOUR BIRD SOUNDS

Volume 1: Songs and Calls of Yard, Garden, and City Birds

Lang Elliott

NatureSound Studio

STACKPOLE BOOKS

Published by
STACKPOLE BOOKS
5067 Ritter Road
Mechanicsburg, PA 17055
www.stackpolebooks.com

Printed in China

10 9 8 7 6 5 4 3 2

This is a revised and expanded edition of the book originally published in 1991 by NatureSound Studio and in 1994 by NorthWord Press.

Photo Credits: Lang Elliott: cover, 12, 22, 24, 26, 32, 36, 38, 46, 50, 52, 58, 60, 66, 68, 70, 74, 76; Marie Read: 10, 14, 18, 20, 30, 34, 40, 44, 56, 62, 72, 78; TomVezo.com: 16, 48; Richard Day: 28, 54; Maslowski Wildlife Productions: 42, 64

Library of Congress Cataloging-in-Publication Data

Elliott, Lang.
  Know your bird sounds / Lang Elliott.
    v. cm.
  "This is a revised and expanded version of the book originally published in 1991 by NatureSound Studio and in 1994 by NorthWord Press"—T.p. verso.
Contents: v. 1. Songs and calls of yard, garden, and city birds.
  ISBN 0-8117-2963-X
  1. Birdsongs. I. Title.
QL698.5 .E4524 2004
598.159—dc22

                                2003024868

ISBN-13: 978-0-8117-2963-5

Contents

Credits and Acknowledgments

Know Your Bird Sounds, Volume One was created and produced by Lang Elliott, owner and operator of NatureSound Studio.

The Sound Recordings: The majority of recordings used in this work were collected in the field by Lang Elliott. Additional recordings were supplied by Bill Evans, Ted Mack, Gene Morton, Gary Ritchison, and the Borror Laboratory of Bioacoustics at Ohio State University.

Sources: Information about sound repertoires was gleaned from the extensive scientific literature. Special thanks to Donald and Lillian Stokes for the sound repertoire summaries and bibliographies provided in their *A Guide to Bird Behavior, Volumes 1–3* (Little, Brown). The Stokes' terminology and functional interpretations were followed whenever appropriate.

Review and Criticism: Bill Evans acted as chief consultant for this production. Details about the repertoires of select species were provided by the following bird sound specialists: Gene Morton (Smithsonian Institution), Gary Ritchison (Eastern Kentucky University), Robert E. Lemon (McGill University), and R. Haven Wiley (University of North Carolina). Although the possibility for errors has been minimized, the author assumes complete responsibility for any identification or classification errors that might eventually become apparent.

*I*magine that it is spring. Darkness gives way to dawn, and the landscape brightens with the sounds of countless birds. Nature's melody flows in through open windows, caresses us with a gentle touch, and refreshes our spirits as we awaken to the new day.

Who has not experienced this tonic effect of bird sound? And who is not moved by the sight and sound of colorful birds, perched atop trees and shrubs, singing excited melodies with heads held high and beaks wide open? During all seasons, listening to the sounds of birds is a joyful and uplifting experience, even when one is totally unaware of the identities of the soundmakers involved.

However, an even richer experience awaits those who explore further— those who develop the ability to identify and understand the varied sounds of familiar birds. When such understanding is obtained, each sound will effortlessly bring forth a vibrant image of the soundmaker, even when it is not visible. Not only will sounds evoke images, they will betray each bird's behavior. Through sound alone, one will know when territorial encounters are in progress, when courtship is taking place, and when predators are threatening nest or young. Stated simply, bird sound provides an excellent doorway into the intimate, personal lives of the birds that surround you.

This unique audio guide presents the basic sound repertoires of thirty-five common birds found in yard, garden, and city settings. Over 150 different types of sounds are included, along with information about their meanings. With the help of this guide, you will move quickly ahead with your personal exploration of the exciting world of bird sound and behavior. Wonderful experiences await you!

Bird Sound Basics

Most of the bird sounds that we hear have evolved as communication signals that transfer useful information from one individual to others of the same species. Some sounds, such as the alarm calls made when a bird swoops at a predator, have obvious effects on other species as well. They irritate the predator, and, at the same time, attract other kinds of birds that join in the effort to drive the predator away.

Certain sounds, while bringing attention to a bird, do not function specifically as communication signals. Examples include the subtle noises made by birds as they hop about in leaves or tap at seeds or nuts. Most wing sounds also fit this category.

One may also distinguish between vocal and nonvocal communication signals. In birds, vocal sounds, or vocalizations, are produced by a specialized internal organ called the syrinx, located low in the bird's windpipe where the trachea first branches. As a general rule, those species with the best-developed syrinxes are capable of producing the most complex sounds. Not surprisingly, the birds we call songbirds (also known as passerines, or perching birds) have the most highly developed vocal organs. Nearly all prominent bird sounds that we hear during typical excursions in the outdoors are vocalizations, and the majority are made by songbirds.

Nonvocal sounds can also function as communication signals. Examples include the drumming of woodpeckers, the specialized wing sounds of pigeons and doves in flight, and the bill-snapping of certain owls. Nonvocal signals are most likely to occur among non-songbirds that have poorly developed syrinxes.

Classification and Functions of Bird Sounds

A mong songbirds, a distinction is made between song and calls. Song is usually a complex auditory signal that is musical or "songlike" to our ears. It is typically produced only by males, and only during the spring and early summer breeding season. Especially during the early hours of the morning, males repeat song after song from prominent perches, in the absence of obvious stimuli.

Song has several functions. First and foremost, it is an expression of territory ownership. By singing, resident males alert other males of the same species that their territory is occupied and likely to be defended. Song also helps unmated males attract mates. And, once mating has occurred, song helps maintain pair bonds by assuring a female that her mate is nearby, and that "all is well."

Technically, the term song applies only to songbirds, but many nonpasserines make sounds that have similar functions. The cooing of the male Mourning Dove is a good example. One may also attribute songlike functions to the whinny call of the Eastern Screech-Owl and the drumming of various woodpeckers.

The term "call," when applied to birds, is broad in definition and includes all utterances that cannot be classified as song. Calls are usually simple in structure. Most are given in response to specific stimuli, and calling bouts are normally short-lived. Many calls are produced by both sexes, and by immature as well as mature birds. Furthermore, calls often occur both inside and outside the breeding season. Given their different criteria, it is usually quite easy to distinguish calls from song. Calls have a variety of functions. There are alarm calls; flocking calls; feeding calls; contact calls; begging calls; aggressive, or agonistic, calls; flight calls; and many others. Some are quite specialized in their use and effect. For instance, the male Eastern Phoebe has a distinct "nest site showing call" that it gives as it flutters in front of a potential nest site when its mate is present nearby.

While bird song draws our attention because of its musical quality, calls actually reveal more about the intimate lives of birds. They alert us to behavior in progress: territorial squabbles, courtship encounters, predator alarm situations, youngsters demanding food, and the like. Without doubt, recognizing calls and their meanings is a crucial step toward gaining a useful appreciation of the languages of the birds.

In this guide, the functions of calls, when they are known, are described briefly in the audio narrative. More detail can be found in the written species accounts. The functions of song are not discussed for each bird because they are more or less the same for all species. Refer to the information presented above if you forget the basic meanings of song.

The Sound Repertoire

The combination of all auditory signals made by a particular species makes up its sound repertoire. This repertoire provides the basic building blocks for the language of the species. Most birds utilize a fixed number of well-defined vocal or nonvocal signals, which they use separately or in combination to bring about communication. In contrast, some birds utilize signals that lie along a continuum, with one call type grading into another in a continuous and gradual manner.

The exact meanings of specific vocal or nonvocal sounds are often difficult to discern. Identical sounds used in different situations may have different effects, and meanings may vary depending on which sex or age class produces or hears a particular sound. Meanings are inferred by the careful study of context—the participants, actions, and reactions that occur in situations where the auditory signals are used.

Scientific studies show that most species have anywhere from several to twenty or more auditory signals that they use to bring about communication. In this guide, the most important and frequently heard elements of each bird's repertoire are emphasized. Certain rare call types are not included, and nestling sounds have been generally excluded. However, great care has been taken to present an auditory sample that truly reflects each bird's soundmaking ability.

O f all the sounds made by songbirds, song attracts the most attention. However, it is interesting to note that certain songbirds lack a clearly defined song. Examples include highly social birds such as the Blue Jay, American Crow, Cedar Waxwing, and Chimney Swift. In these species, males and females look alike, individuals often feed together in groups, and breeding pairs are not clearly territorial. Apparently, song is not necessary to assure breeding success in these species.

The majority of songbirds do sing, but the details of song structure and delivery vary tremendously from species to species. As a rule, the songs of any one species are quite distinct from the songs of other species. These "species-specific" differences allow us humans (and the birds) to confidently use songs as species identifiers, even when singers are not actually seen.

Some species have simple and call-like songs that vary little between individuals. For instance, male Eastern Phoebes repeatedly sing a buzzy *fee-beee . . . fee-beee . . .* for minutes on end. Phoebe song is very stereotyped, and the songs of different individuals are difficult, if not impossible, to distinguish.

In contrast, certain other species have complex and musical songs that they repeat with only minor variation. The Baltimore Oriole is a good example. Each individual sings musical but stereotyped songs that vary slightly in length. Interestingly, different individuals often have different-sounding songs. Nonetheless, the songs of all males of the species possess a common "oriole quality" that makes them easy to recognize as Baltimore Oriole songs, in spite of their variability.

Song Sparrows show a more complicated pattern. Individuals have ten or more different song types in their repertoire. They sing one type for several minutes, and then switch to another. Furthermore, individuals tend to possess a number of unique songs, making it possible for males to actually recognize specific neighbors, based entirely on the individuality of their songs.

Catbirds, mockingbirds, and thrashers fit yet another category. They sing long, continuous songs made up of a great variety of phrases. Each individual has a vocabulary consisting of a large number of phrase types that it combines in countless ways to produce a song pattern that seems continuously variable and ever-changing.

Clearly, there is considerable variation in the details of singing behavior among songbirds. Each species must be studied carefully before its pattern can be described and understood.

SPECIAL TYPES OF SONG

The typical song of a species may be termed its territorial song. This is the type of song we are most likely to hear during excursions outdoors. However, under certain circumstances birds may sing special songs that sound different from typical song.

For instance, a variety of birds have a dawn song, or twilight song, that they sing during the hour before sunrise. The Purple Martin is a good example. Males sing a distinctive dawn song that sounds quite different from their normal song. The primary function of dawn song in martins and other species is not clearly understood.

Another special song is aggressive song, usually given when an excited male is involved in a territorial encounter. While most birds simply increase the cadence of their singing in such situations, species such as the Yellow Warbler (covered in Volume 2) sing a noticeably different song type that betrays their aggressive mood.

During the height of courtship, a male may approach a female and sing an excited, continuous courtship song that often leads to copulation. Species showing this behavior include several backyard favorites: the House Finch, Purple Finch, and House Wren.

Yet another special song type is flight song, often given as males flutter slowly upward in what is termed "moth flight." Birds that sing rather typical songs in flight include the Northern Mockingbird, Purple Finch, and Song Sparrow. In contrast, the Common Yellowthroat (covered in Volume 2) sings a unique flight song that is noticeably different from typical song. The Purple Martin's dawn song, described above, also qualifies as flight song because it is sung by flying birds.

Among temperate zone songbirds, song is usually restricted to males. However, female song occurs in some species. Female Northern Cardinals, Baltimore Orioles, Tufted Titmice, and Common Grackles sing songs that sound much like those of the males. In other species, such as the Red-winged

Blackbird (covered in Volume 2), females have a songlike vocalization that sounds entirely different from the male's song.

COUNTER-SINGING, SONG-MATCHING, AND DUETTING

During territorial encounters, neighboring individuals of a given species may sing back and forth in an alternating fashion—a phenomenon known as counter-singing. When such clear alternation is heard, one can be reasonably certain that the birds involved are paying close attention to one another. The Northern Cardinal and Tufted Titmouse are species that commonly demonstrate counter-singing behavior.

A related phenomenon is song-matching, also heard among cardinals and titmice. In both of these species, individuals have song repertoires consisting of several different song patterns. During bouts of counter-singing, the participating birds often "match songs" by converging upon the same or similar patterns. Not surprisingly, song-matching and counter-singing often go hand-in-hand.

In the tropics, a variety of species demonstrate song-duetting, where both members of a pair sing together in a close-knit fashion. Song-duetting is rare among temperate zone birds, but some species show related forms of duetting. For instance, during territorial encounters, female Carolina Wrens chatter when their mates sing. Similarly, Brown-headed Cowbird females often make a harsh sputtering call just as the male sings. Duetting probably helps strengthen pair bonds and may send a strong territorial message to potential intruders.

VOCAL IMITATION

It is well-known that certain species of wild birds imitate the sounds of other species. Usually, they insert imitations into their songs, mixing them with their own sounds. The Northern Mockingbird and European Starling are superb imitators. Catbirds and thrashers also show this behavior, and Blue Jays often imitate the calls of native hawks.

The function of vocal imitation remains unclear. However, our native imitators do allow us to test our ability to identify common bird sounds. Listen carefully to the songs of mockingbirds and starlings and see how many imitations you can recognize. The greater your knowledge of bird sound, the more imitations you will hear!

Remembering Bird Sounds

A useful aid to remembering bird sounds is to fix a name to each sound. In this guide, care has been taken to give each sound a name that accurately describes the sound. A reference list of sound categories is provided at the end of this book. After you're somewhat familiar with the bird sounds presented, use the list to test your memory of each bird's repertoire and the names of the various calls.

Some names are onomatopoeic, that is, pronouncing the word or phrase imitates the actual sound. Onomatopoeic "memory phrases" are a great aid to remembering certain bird sounds. For example, the nonsense phrase *fee-bee-fee-bay* describes the tonal changes in a Carolina Chickadee's song, and *teakettle, teakettle, teakettle* indicates the cadence of the Carolina Wren's song. Likewise, words or letter groups like *chip, churr, tsk,* and *bzzz,* when pronounced, actually sound like specific bird calls.

Certain names, such as the robin's "whinny call," liken the actual sound to a reference sound with which we are familiar—in this case, the whinny of a horse. Still other names, such as "whining call" or "whistle call," refer to a well-known category or quality of sound. In some instances, the function of a sound is used to create a name: "mobbing call," "nest alarm call," "nest site showing call," and so forth.

Memorizing the names of sounds and associating them with images seen in bird guides is a useful learning technique. But the best learning style of all is to immerse yourself in direct outdoor observation. When you have actually heard sounds in natural settings, and seen the soundmakers in action, the sounds and sights together will make a lasting impression and you will have little trouble remembering them. While this guide can give form and structure to your outdoor explorations, the outdoor experience itself should be your final and ultimate goal. Happy listening!

Sounds of Yard, Garden, and City Birds

1. American Robin

O ne of the most abundant, widespread, and well-known North American birds, the American Robin (10 inches long) is easily recognized by its brick-red breast set against its slate-gray back and head. A member of the thrush family, the robin frequents a variety of habitats, including residential areas, city parks, and farmland, as well as forested areas and mountain lands.

Typical Song (males only): In spring and summer, males sing a melodic, whistled song composed of groups of variable phrases separated by distinct pauses. *Cheerily, cheerup, cheerio, cheerily,* the male seems to say, before pausing and singing again.

Continuous Song (males only): Especially at dawn, males often sing an excited version of song that lacks the pauses between phrases that are evident in typical song.

Peek and *Tut* Calls (both sexes): In alarm situations, especially during the nesting season, robins of both sexes respond with sharp *peek* calls and softer *tut* notes. These calls are often given in rough alternation.

Whinny Call (both sexes): Robins sometimes produce an excited outburst of notes that sounds similar to the whinny of a small horse. The first notes in the series are usually the loudest, and a drop in pitch occurs about halfway through. The whinny seems to be given in situations of mild alarm.

High *Seeee* Call (both sexes?): A penetrating, high-pitched *seeee* is given in response to the presence of an aerial predator, especially during the nesting season when young are near. Although considered a "hawk alarm call," this vocalization may be given in other alarm situations. It is delivered with beak wide open.

Zeeeup! Call (both sexes): Especially during migration, robins periodically make a buzzy *zeeee!*, or *zeeeup!* This call probably functions as a contact note. It is often given in flight.

*T*he Northern Cardinal (8 inches long) is a favorite neighborhood song-ster named for the brilliant cardinal-red color of the male. The female is pale brown with some red on her wings. Both sexes have prominent crests. Cardinals may be observed year-round in back yards, city parks, woodlots, and forested areas.

Song (both sexes): Cardinal song is made up of clear, slurred whistles, usu-ally sung in repeated groups. Each bird has a vocabulary of several phrase-types that it combines to produce a number of different songs. Common phrases sound like *purdy, purdy, purdy . . . whoit, whoit, whoit . . .* or *what-cheer, what-cheer*. Rarely, songs end with a soft, rattling *churr*. Females occasionally sing and often alternate songs with their mate.

***Chip* Call (both sexes):** In alarm situations and a variety of other circum-stances, cardinals make high, metallic *chip*s. These calls may be given singly, repeated slowly, or else delivered in rapid volleys or "chitters." The *chip* is the cardinal's most common call.

***Chuck* or *Kwut* Call (both sexes):** A harsh *chuck* or *kwut* is given by cardi-nals during courtship interactions, aggressive encounters, and situations where nest or young are threatened. This call probably indicates a high state of arousal.

***Chip-kwut* Call (both sexes):** During aggressive interactions, cardinals often give high *chip*s and low *kwut*s in rapid alternation: *chip-kwut, chip-kwut, chip-kwut . . .* To some, this call sounds more like *pee-too, pee-too, pee-too . . .*

Other Calls: Especially during courtship interactions, cardinals mix song fragments with various calls. Sometimes, a harsh *churr* is prominent. This same *churr* rarely follows song (see above).

3. Baltimore Oriole

*T*he Baltimore Oriole (8 inches long) is one of our most colorful yard and garden birds. The male is bright orange below, black above, and sports a solid black head and black wing bars. The female is olive-green above and yellow below. This migrant species nests in tall shade trees. The oriole's pendulous, socklike nest is distinctive.

Song (both sexes): The song of the Baltimore Oriole is made up of rich, slurred whistles that have a distinctive quality that is easy to learn. Some songs contain one or more harsh notes. Each bird has a rather stereotyped song pattern but may vary song length. Females occasionally sing during the courtship phase.

Whistle Calls (both sexes): Single-note, double-note, or three-note whistles are given by orioles in a variety of situations and may serve as contact calls. Such whistles often occur between songs and might be considered song fragments.

Rapid Chatter and *Gee-gee* Calls (both sexes): When alarmed or otherwise aroused, orioles produce harsh, scolding calls. One type, often given during encounters between orioles, is a variable *gee-gee-gee-gee*. Another common arousal call is a harsh, rapid chatter, often given when the nest is threatened. These two call types seem to intergrade.

Fledgling Calls (both sexes): After leaving the nest, immature orioles make loud, nasal calls sounding like *dee-dee-dee-dee*. These calls are thought to alert the parents to the whereabouts of youngsters and stimulate them to bring food.

4. Orchard Oriole

The Orchard Oriole ($6^1/_2$ inches long) is a darker version of the Baltimore Oriole. Underparts are a deep chestnut-orange, with black head, back, and tail. The female is olive-green above and yellowish below. Orchard Orioles are common in the Midwest and South, where they frequent open groves and enliven their surroundings with their jumbled, warbling song. Immature males resemble females but have a black throat.

Song (males only): Male song is a rapid series of varied, whistled notes that sometimes include buzzes or trills. There is often a harsh, down-slurred phrase at the end. Individuals have a vocabulary of twenty or more phrases that they combine in different ways to make different-sounding songs.

Chatter Call (both sexes): In alarm situations, Orchard Orioles produce a prolonged, harsh chatter reminiscent of the chatter of the Baltimore Oriole, but higher in pitch.

***Chuck, Chuck-seet!,* and Whistle Calls (both sexes?):** A common call of the Orchard Oriole is a short *chuck*, similar in quality to the calls of grackles or blackbirds. Sometimes, the *chuck* is followed by a sudden whistled note: *chuck-seet*! On occasion, clear whistles are produced that sound much like the whistles of a Baltimore Oriole. The functions of these calls are not known.

5. Tufted Titmouse

An eastern forest species that has adapted well to neighborhood settings is the Tufted Titmouse (6 inches long). Gray above and light below, the titmouse's distinguishing feature is its tufted crest. The sexes look alike. Omnivorous in diet, titmice eat insects, berries, and seeds. They hold seeds under their feet on branches and hack them open with their bills.

Song (both sexes): The typical song of the titmouse is a clear, whistled *peeto, peeto, peeto,* or a down-slurred *peeyer, peeyer,* repeated several times. Individuals have several song types in their repertoire, and often sing one type for several minutes before changing to another. Neighboring males often counter-sing and match their song patterns. Odd song types are commonplace. One distinctive pattern sounds like *keep!-her,* dropping in pitch at the end. Titmouse songs are often confused with the songs of Northern Cardinals and Carolina Wrens.

Jway-jway Call (both sexes): During aggressive encounters and alarm situations, titmice make raspy *jway* calls, which they usually repeat several times. This call is variable, but easily recognized.

Tsickajwee Call (both sexes): Another common call of the titmouse, given during aggressive encounters and other situations of excitement, sounds like *tsickajwee* or *tsickajwee-jwee.* This call is often confused with the *chicka-dee-dee* call of chickadees.

Tseep Call (both sexes): The contact call of the titmouse is a short, high-pitched *tseep,* given by foraging birds year-round.

High Seeee Call-Series (both sexes): A series of very high-pitched whistles, *seee-seee-seee-seee* . . . , is given by males during territorial conflicts and by mates involved in courtship or copulation.

6. Black-capped Chickadee

The acrobatic Black-capped Chickadee (5 inches long) is a favorite visitor to bird feeders across the northern half of the continent. Named in part for its black cap, the chickadee is gray above, light below, and has a distinctive black bib. The sexes look alike. Black-caps are active little birds that are year-round residents in open woods and forest edges. They derive the last part of their name from their common call, *chicka-dee-dee*.

Song (males only): The Black-cap's melodic song is a clear, whistled *feee-bee-ee*. The first note is more highly pitched than the last two, which are on the same pitch. Quite often, the terminal notes are slurred together and songs sound two-parted: *feee-beee*.

Chicka-dee-dee Calls (both sexes): Chickadees get their name from their common flocking call, *chicka-dee-dee-dee*, given at various tempos. This call occurs frequently outside the breeding season, and is often given by individuals separated from winter foraging flocks.

Tseet Call (both sexes): The contact call of the Black-cap is a high *tseet*, often given by members of a flock, family, or pair.

Gargle Calls (both sexes): A rapid, gargling sputter of notes sounding like *tseedleedeet* or *t'slink-rrrrr* is given by chickadees during aggressive encounters, especially during chases. Gargle calls are highly variable, but clearly distinct from other chickadee calls.

High Chatter (both sexes): A high-pitched series of rapidly delivered notes sounding like *chippychippychippychip* is often given by a dominant chickadee after he displaces another from a feeder or other food source.

High Seee Call-Series (both sexes): A rapid, prolonged series of variable, high-pitched *seee* calls are made by chickadees in response to predators, or during conflict situations and courtship.

7. Carolina Chickadee

Very similar in appearance to the Black-capped Chickadee, the Carolina Chickadee (5 inches long) replaces it in the southeastern states. While there is some interbreeding in areas of overlap, the two species are most reliably separated by range or by song. This southern chickadee visits bird feeders, but less so than its northern relative. Its calls are similar to those of the Black-cap.

Song (males only): The typical song of the Carolina Chickadee is a four-note, whistled *fee-bee-fee-bay*. The first note is the highest. The second is lower than the first. The third note is higher than the second but lower than the first. And the fourth and final note is the lowest of all. Song structure is variable; some songs contain only two or three notes and others have as many as five or six.

***Chicka-dee-dee* Calls (both sexes):** The *chicka-dee-dee* call of the Carolina Chickadee typically has more terminal *dee* notes and a more rapid delivery than the same call given by Black-caps. It occurs in alarm situations, but also seems to function as a flocking call.

***Seep* Calls (both sexes):** High-pitched *seep* calls are given by individuals of both sexes during foraging and in a variety of other situations. They are considered contact notes.

Raspy Gargle Calls (both sexes): A variety of raspy, sputtering gargle calls are given in aggressive situations. They indicate an attack tendency. Some sound like *tseedleedeet* or *tseedelink*, and others have a burry ending: *tseedleeburrrr*.

Harsh Chatter (both sexes): Especially during aggressive disputes, Carolina Chickadees produce a rapid chatter of harsh, high-pitched notes.

High *Seee* Call-Series (both sexes): A rapid series of high and thin *seee* calls are given in a variety of breeding related situations and also during aggressive encounters. The rambling notes making up the series often vary considerably in pitch.

8. White-breasted Nuthatch

A common visitor to feeders, the White-breasted Nuthatch (5 inches long) is a stubby little bird with a square cut tail and a slender beak. Both sexes are gray above and white below. The male has a black cap; the female's cap is gray. Nuthatches search for insects in bark crevices by spiraling around branches like tiny wind-up toys, often hanging upside down or walking headfirst down tree trunks.

Yank and Yank-yank Calls (both sexes): The most common call of the white-breasted nuthatch is a nasal *yank*, often given in pairs: *yank-yank*. This call indicates mild excitement and probably functions as a long-distance contact call.

Excited Yank-Series (both sexes): An excited series of *yank* calls are given in situations of alarm, especially when predators threaten nest or young.

Ik Notes (both sexes): While foraging, members of a pair or family group communicate with soft calls sounding like *ik* or *ip*. These contact calls are sometimes given in pairs, with the second note sounding slightly different from the first: *ik . . . uck*.

Song (males only): The song of the male, given mostly in late winter or early spring, is a rapid series of slightly musical, nasal notes, delivered at various rates: *hey-hey-hey-hey-hey . . .*

Whining Calls, including Pheeoo (both sexes): Adult and immature nuthatches make peculiar, whining notes in a variety of circumstances. A distinctive, down-slurred *pheeoo* may indicate anxiety, but it is also repeated by both sexes during sexual chases and encounters involving copulation.

9. House Wren

The most widespread and common of our native wrens is the small and energetic House Wren (5 inches long), a plain brown species with a short tail that it often holds cocked. The spring arrival of this migrant is marked by the activity of the bubbly male as he builds stick nests in a variety of cavities to woo females. A prospective mate eventually selects one in which to lay her eggs.

Song (males only): The male's song is a rich, melodious, and bubbling series of exuberantly delivered notes. It starts slowly, rises in volume and pitch, then drops at the end in a rapid cascade of notes. The male often points his tail downward when singing.

Shrill Song (male only): In the presence of a female, the courting male House Wren sings an excited, continuous version of song known as shrill song. As he courts, he quivers his wings and sings energetically, alternating typical song phrases with high, squealing notes that betray his high level of sexual excitement.

***Chit* and *Churrr* Calls (both sexes):** In a variety of alarm situations, House Wrens respond with sharp *chit* calls and more drawn-out *churrr*s. *Chit*s may be given in a rapid series, and both calls may be combined to produce *churrr-chit*s.

Rattle Call (both sexes): Another alarm call, given especially when a predator threatens nest or young, is a harsh, extended rattle, which is repeated time and again until the danger passes. The rattle call may intergrade with the rapid *chit*-series.

Buzz Call (both sexes?): Another House Wren call is a snarling series of short buzzy sounds, apparently given in response to predators. This call is distinct from other House Wren calls.

10. Carolina Wren

Our largest native wren is the Carolina Wren (5¹/₂ inches long), recognized by its reddish brown upper parts, white eye stripe, and warm buff flanks. This species is found year-round over much of the East. Carolina Wrens prefer thick undergrowth, where they dart about in search of insects and other arthropods.

Song (males only): The loud, ringing song of the male is a rapidly repeated series of up to twelve identical phrases. Each bird has a repertoire of a number of different phrase patterns, and usually sings one pattern for several minutes before changing to another. Useful verbalizations include: *teakettle-teakettle-teakettle* . . . and *cheery-cheery-cheery* . . .

***Cheer* Call and *P'dink* (males only):** In alarm situations, including territorial disputes, males in northern populations respond with a burry, down-slurred *cheer*. In contrast, males in southern populations respond with a ringing *pink* or *p'dink*.

Paired *Dits* (females only): Especially during territorial encounters, but also in the presence of predators, female Carolina Wrens produce a pair of notes sounding like *dit-dit*. At least in northern populations, females commonly alternate this call with their mate's *cheer* calls.

Female Chatter (females only): During territorial encounters involving male song, the female often follows or overlaps her mate's song with a distinctive, harsh chatter.

Raspy *Churr* Call (both sexes?): In the presence of predators, and in other alarm situations, aroused individuals produce raspy *churr*s that they repeat as long as danger is present.

11. Cedar Waxwing

The Cedar Waxing (7 inches long) is an elegant, crested species identified by its brown color, the black line through its eyes, and the prominent yellow band on the tip of its tail. The sexes look alike. Waxwings get their name from the waxy-looking red tips on some of the wing feathers. They prefer to eat berries. During courtship, members of a pair will pass a berry back and forth until one finally eats it.

Hissy *Seeee* Calls (both sexes): High-pitched, drawn-out whistles, or hissy *seeee* calls, are given by waxwings in a variety of situations. They often occur just before flying, when taking flight, or during flight, but may also be given by perched birds.

Buzzy Trills (both sexes): Cedar Waxwings also make high, buzzy trills, *bzeee . . . bzeee*, which sound quite different from hissy *seeee* calls. Trills are usually given by perched birds, but may also occur in flight. This is the primary call of immature waxwings.

Rapid Trill Sequence (both sexes): During food-begging by excited fledglings, and when females beg during courtship, short, buzzy trills are given in rapid succession: *bzee-bzee-bzee . . .*

The Gray Catbird (9 inches long) frequents residential areas but often passes unnoticed due to its drab color and preference for dense shrubbery. It can be identified by its long tail, slate gray color, and black cap, and by the chestnut patch under its tail. The catbird is named for its nasal catlike *mew* call, which may be interspersed with song.

Song (males only): The song of the male is a continued series of variable phrases. Each phrase is almost always different from the one that precedes it. Some are musical in effect and others are harsh and discordant. Compared with the songs of thrashers and mockingbirds, the catbird's performance sounds high-pitched and squeaky. Soft *mew* calls are often interspersed in song, and some phrases may be imitations of sounds made by other birds.

Mew Calls (both sexes): Catbirds respond to a variety of alarm situations with harsh *mews* likened to the meows of house cats. Soft *mews* probably indicate mild arousal. Extremely upset birds give loud and emphatic versions.

Kwut Calls (both sexes): Another catbird alarm call is a throaty *kwut*, usually delivered in a series. *Kwut*s seem to be given primarily in situations that threaten nest or young.

Ratchet Call (both sexes): A rather unusual call of the catbird is a sudden, ratchetlike *tch-tch-tch-tch*. This call is often made by birds startled into flight, but may also be given by perched birds. Ratchet calls probably indicate alarm.

Generally secretive, the Brown Thrasher (11 inches long) is a sight to behold when it is perched atop a tree singing in the springtime. Rufous-brown above and heavily streaked below, the thrasher resembles a Wood Thrush, but is larger and has a down-curved beak, a long tail, and yellow eyes. It nests and feeds in thickets and shrubs and usually stays well hidden in dense tangles. The Brown Thrasher has a distinctive song, composed of doubled phrases.

Song (males only): The thrasher's long-continued song is brighter and more melodic than the catbird's song. It is composed of variable phrases, but can be recognized because many phrases are repeated two and sometimes three times. Song may include imitations of sounds made by other birds.

***Smack!* Call (both sexes):** A common alarm call of the thrasher is a loud, kisslike *smack!* given in a variety of arousal situations. *Smack!*s are sometimes delivered as a rapid pair—*smack-smack!*—which resembles the ratchet call of the catbird.

Burry *Teeooo* Call (both sexes): Another thrasher alarm call, given especially when nest or young are threatened, is a burry, down-slurred *teeooo*, often given along with *smack!* calls. *Teeooo* calls probably indicate a high level of arousal.

Harsh *Chjjj* Call (both sexes): Thrashers make distinctive harsh calls sounding like *chjjjj*. These calls are given when birds go to roost at dusk or before they leave their roost at dawn. *Chjjj* calls may also occur during social encounters.

14. Northern Mockingbird

K nown for its remarkable ability to imitate the sounds of other birds, the Northern Mockingbird (about 10 inches long) is dull gray above, pale below, and has white patches on its wings that are evident in flight. The sexes look alike. This abundant and conspicuous year-round resident of the South is expanding northward into the Midwest and Northeast. Aggressive near its nest, mockingbirds chase away other birds and may also swoop at dogs, cats, and humans.

Song (both sexes): The mockingbird's song is long-continued and sounds much like the thrasher's song. However, individual phrase-types are often repeated three or more times in succession. Some phrases are rich and melodic, while others are harsh or staccato in quality. Mockingbirds insert many excellent imitations of other bird sounds into their songs. They sometimes sing while flying from perch to perch. Females also sing, mostly in the fall as they set up winter feeding territories.

***Chewk* Call (both sexes):** Especially at dusk, mockingbirds make harsh, burry *chewk* calls, which they repeat once every few seconds. Although given in certain alarm situations, *chewk* calls may aid in the formation and maintenance of winter territories. Immature birds also make these calls.

Harsh *Chjjj* Call (both sexes): Courting mockingbirds make soft, harsh *chjjj* calls as they follow one another about. This intimate call is pitched slightly higher than the thrasher's very similar vocalization.

***Chitichick!* Call (both sexes):** A rapid series of harsh notes sounding like *chitichick!* is made by mockingbirds as they chase other species of birds from their winter territories. This call is also given in encounters with other mockingbirds.

15. Blue Jay

*T*he noisy and raucous Blue Jay (12 inches long) is known for its aggressive disposition around bird feeders, where it chases away other species. It is bright blue above, grayish below; it has a prominent crest, a black necklace, and white and black patterns on wings and tail. Jays are year-round residents throughout the East and Midwest.

Jay and *Jay-jay* **Calls (both sexes):** Individuals of both sexes make highly variable nasal calls sounding like *jay* or *jay-jay*. This all-purpose call is the Blue Jay's most common sound. It may be used as a contact call or flocking call. It may indicate alarm. And it is commonly used when jays excitedly heckle hawks, owls, or other predators.

Tool-ool, Tweedlee, **and** *Squeakly-squeak* **(both sexes?):** Blue Jays make an incredible variety of sounds, and little is known about their functions. Quite frequently, they make melodic and piping *toots* or two-parted calls sounding like *tool-ool*. Another common pattern sounds like *tweedlee* or *toodleloo*. One interesting jay call type reminds many of a squeaky gate or pump-handle: *squeakly-squeak*. Quite often, the soundmaker bobs up and down as the sounds are produced. Some of these sounds, especially those given by flocking jays in the spring, are thought to be associated with courtship.

Comb Call (both sexes): Blue Jays make a unique clicking call reminding one of the sound made by drawing a fingernail across the teeth of a plastic comb. This comb call, which is thought to be associated with courtship, is sometimes accompanied by bobbing. It occurs along with other calls when groups of individuals congregate in treetops in late winter or spring.

Kew **Calls and Subtle Whines (both sexes):** An intimate sound made by members of a pair or a family group is a nasal *kew, kew*. Other intimate sounds include expressive whining notes that can only be heard from a short distance.

Hawk Imitations (both sexes): Blue Jays commonly imitate the calls of various hawks, especially the Red-shouldered Hawk, Red-tailed Hawk, and Broad-winged Hawk. Interestingly, these imitations often give the impression that a distant hawk is vocalizing, even when the Blue Jay is nearby. The function of hawk imitations is not known.

16. American Crow

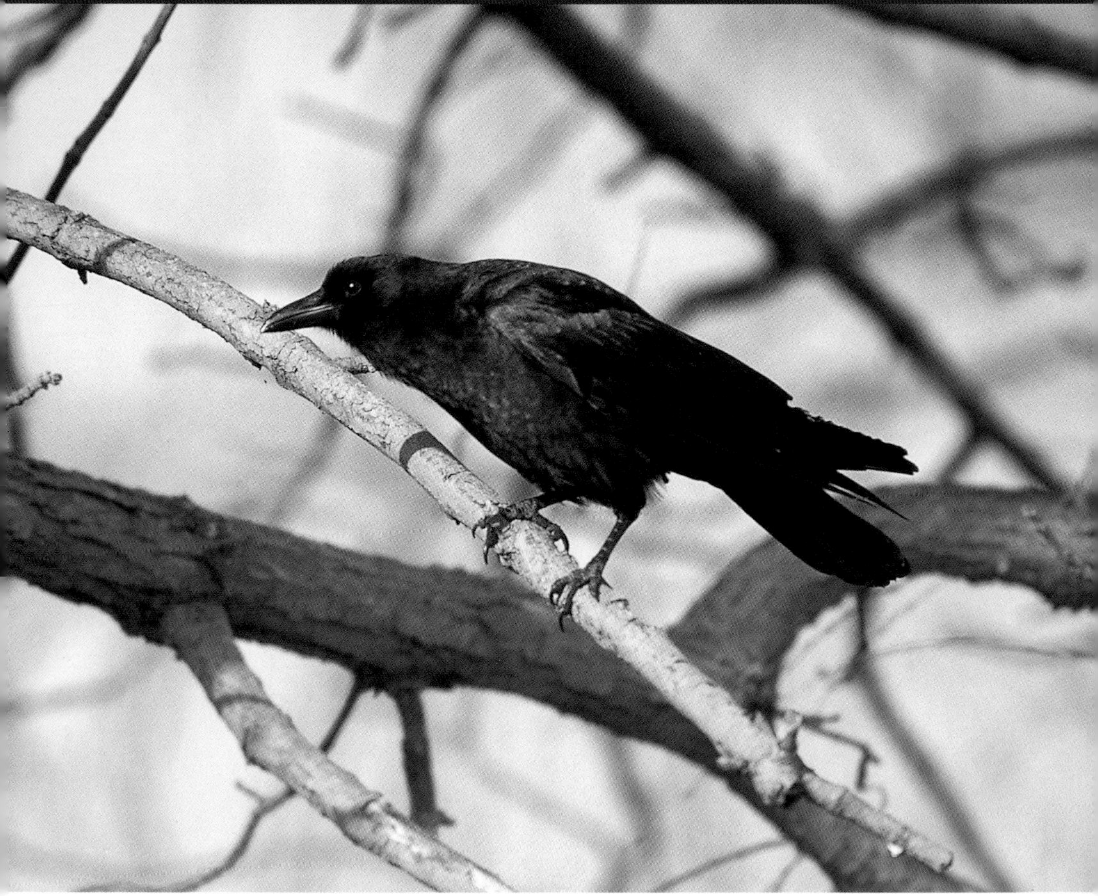

*T*he largest and most widespread of our native crows is the American Crow (about 20 inches long), an all-black bird with a long, heavy bill. This well-known species is common in a variety of habitats across North America. It is a year-round resident in most areas, but does migrate in the northernmost part of its range. Crows are highly gregarious outside the breeding season and often roost at night in large flocks.

Caw! Call (both sexes): The most common sound made by crows is a raucous, throaty *caw!* given singly, in pairs, or in a rapid series. Crows are incredibly expressive in their use of this basic sound, which they adapt to the situation at hand. Well over a dozen variations have been defined. Loud, excited *caws!* are given as crows heckle or mob predators such as hawks, owls, or house cats. Vocalizing birds swoop at the predator, and, in the case of flying birds of prey, chase them through the air.

Juvenile Nasal Calls (both sexes): Young crows make calls that sound less harsh and more nasal than adult calls: a mellow *cah*, rather than a raucous *caw!* When an adult approaches, a juvenile may call excitedly in hopes of getting fed.

Growling Sounds (both sexes): Low-pitched growling sounds are sometimes made by crows, usually during disputes over food.

Rattle Call (both sexes): A very distinctive crow call, given by perched or flying birds, is a dry rattle. If made by a perched bird, the rattle is accompanied by bobbing. Flying birds often rattle while diving or swooping in the air. Rattles are most often heard in the spring and are thought to be associated with courtship.

Unusual Crow Sounds (both sexes): In intimate situations involving pairs or family members, crows make odd, uncrowlike sounds. For instance, a soft, bell-like *too-doo, too-doo* is given as a greeting display. Another unusual call sounds like *crrracko, crrracko*. Its function is not known.

The only swift in the East, the blackish Chimney Swift (5 inches long) circles about high in the air capturing insects on the wing. It is easily recognized by its small, cigar-shaped body and stiff pointed wings. Chimney Swifts roost in chimneys, where they may be seen in great numbers at dusk whirling about and making high-pitched chattering calls before descending into the chimney for the night.

Chitter Call (both sexes): The Chimney Swift's most common call is a series of high-pitched notes run together to produce a rapid chitter: *chipichipichipichip*. Chitters are given by flying birds in a variety of situations and may serve as general contact calls. In late summer, when swifts gather prior to migration, large groups may be observed circling abandoned chimneys at dusk, chittering excitedly before entering for the night.

Chip **Series (both sexes):** In the spring, groups of three birds are often seen flying together in a tight formation. These "trio flights" are thought to be a courtship ceremony where two males vie for a single female. During such flights, at least one participant quickly repeats high-pitched *chip* calls until the trio flight ends.

A lso known as the familiar urban pigeon, the Rock Dove (13 inches long) originally hailed from Europe to North Africa and India. It is now found throughout most of North America and comes in a variety of color variants, though most are grayish with a whitish rump, black wing bars, and iridescent green and purple on the neck. Male Rock Doves court females by puffing out their necks, wheeling about, and making a gurgling, cooing sound.

Display Coo (given primarily by males): The most complex Rock Dove vocalization is the display coo, a call sounding like *coo-roo-c'too-coo*. It is given along with the "bowing display," in which a pigeon bows and turns round and round with throat inflated and tail spread. This display is used to threaten rivals of either sex, and is also performed in front of females prior to mounting and copulation. Females periodically give the display coo.

Perch Coo or Moan (both sexes): Around nesting areas, individuals of both sexes (especially males) produce a low, moaning *aoo, aoo, aoo, aoo* . . . The male uses this call to advertise his availability to a potential mate. Female moans are thought to reduce male aggression and strengthen the pair bond.

Wing Clapping and Whirring (both sexes): Upon taking flight, pigeons of both sexes make sharp, clapping noises with their wings. This sound is accentuated in sexually active birds, especially in males. They clap loudly and then glide with wings held up—a mate attraction display. Flying pigeons also make distinctive whirring sounds with their wings.

19. Mourning Dove

*T*he most common and widespread of our native doves is the slim, fast-flying Mourning Dove (12 inches long), a species ranging across most of the country. Both sexes are gray to pinkish gray and have long, pointed tails tipped with white. Doves are year-round residents over most of their range and can be seen perched on telephone lines or searching for seeds on the ground below bird feeders.

Long Coo (males; rarely females): The breeding call of the Mourning Dove, given with throat inflated, is a long, owl-like coo: *hooo-waoo-hooo-hoo-hoo*. Unmated males use long coos to attract mates. This call also occurs during territorial encounters. On rare occasions, females make a weak version of this sound.

Short Coo (both sexes): A short version of the coo, *hooo-waoo*, is given by both sexes. It is most common early in the breeding season. Males use short coos to attract females to nest sites, and females often give short coos from the nest. This call may also occur during courtship and territorial encounters.

Wing Twitter (both sexes): When flying, and especially when startled into flight, doves often produce a whistling or twittering sound with their wings. This sound probably communicates alarm. Doves can also fly without making the twittering sound.

Common but easily overlooked, the Eastern Screech-Owl (8 1/2 inches long) frequents suburban woodlots and parks as well as more remote forests and swamps. Possessing small ear tufts, screech-owls occur in both red and gray color morphs. Surprisingly, they rarely screech. Their common calls include a descending whinny and a soft trill. Screech-Owls nest in tree hollows.

Whinny Call (both sexes): Screech-owls produce an eerie, wavering whistle that drops in pitch and sounds like the whinny of a small horse. This call may serve as a long-distance territorial call. It is most commonly heard in late summer and autumn. Short, monotonic trills may be given along with whinnies.

Monotonic Trill (both sexes): Another common call of the screech-owl is a low, quickening, melodic trill that stays on one pitch and lasts up to about five seconds. This call is softly delivered and has a ventriloquial quality, making it difficult to locate vocalizing individuals, even when they are nearby. Trills are usually given during social encounters when individuals are close to one another. Sometimes, members of a pair or family group alternate and/or overlap monotonic trills to produce a pleasing effect. The trill of the female is slightly longer and more highly pitched than the male's trill. Juvenile trills are higher and harsher than adult trills.

Alarm Whines and Bill-Snapping (both sexes): When nest or young are threatened, screech-owls respond with down-slurred whines. Alarmed birds also snap their bills in protest, a behavior thought to frighten or confuse predators.

With rapid, blurred wingbeats, the Ruby-throated Hummingbird (3 1/2 inches long) visits garden flowers to sip nectar with its long, needlelike beak. Both sexes are metallic green above and pale below. The male has an iridescent red throat and a forked tail; the female's tail is blunt. The ruby-throat prefers red tubular flowers, where it finds nectar and small insects. Its tiny, cup-shaped nest is covered with bits of lichen held together with silken strands from spider webs.

Squeaky *Chips* (both sexes): While flying or hovering, Ruby-throats make squeaky *chips*, especially in crowded situations around a food source. *Chips* may be given in rapid succession. They probably indicate mild arousal in competitive situations.

Chase Calls and High *Tseeps* (both sexes?): During aggressive chases, the dominant individual makes a distinctive chase call while chasing the rival away: *tseep-beurr-chippitychip*. High *tseep* notes (indicating aggression) may also be given, and wing-boxing may precede chases.

Wing-Boxing (both sexes?): When an aggressor first attacks a rival, their beating wings often make physical contact, producing a papery, crackling sound. A chase usually follows.

Pendulum Arc Buzz and Related Displays (both sexes): As a territorial and courtship display, males fly back and forth in a regular fashion along a swinglike arc that varies in length from several feet to twenty feet or more. At the bottom of each arc, the male produces a sudden wing hum or buzz that may include a high-pitched, rattling twitter. Sometimes, the arc is short and almost horizontal, and the swinging motion may have an irregular tempo. Often, a prospective mate or rival is perched nearby. Females are known to give versions of this display. On occasion, pairs face one another and then fly up and down in a see-saw manner while making a rattling, buzzy twitter.

The Red-bellied Woodpecker (9 inches long) is recognized by the black-and-white bars on its wing, back, and tail, its tan neck and belly, and the red on the back of its neck. In the male, the red patch extends to the forehead. This woodpecker is misleadingly named because the slight wash of red on the belly is usually not visible in the field. The Red-belly is primarily a bird of the Southeast, where its vibrant call enlivens swamp and forest settings.

Querr Call (both sexes): The Red-belly's most conspicuous call is a rolling, nasal *querr*, often given in pairs: *querr-querr*. This call occurs in a variety of situations, sometimes in the absence of an obvious stimulus. It probably functions as a contact note, and perhaps a territorial call.

Drumming (both sexes): During the breeding season, individuals of both sexes pound their beaks against resonant wood to produce a loud drumming sound. The drumming of the Red-belly has an even tempo and lasts about one second or less. Drumming helps individuals advertise territory and attract mates. It may also serve to maintain pair bonds once breeding has commenced.

Chi Call and Chatter-chi (both sexes): Another common call is an emphatic *chi* that may be excitedly repeated. The *chi* call seems to convey mild arousal or alarm. A related call is the chatter-*chi*, a rapid volley of *chi* calls, given during social encounters and often followed by flight. Excited *chi* calling often leads up to a chatter-*chi*.

Harsh Churr and Woika-woika (both sexes?): During social encounters, individuals make harsh *churr*s that sound noticeably different from *querr* calls. Another distinctive encounter call sounds like *woika-woika-woika . . .* These and other Red-belly calls accompany courtship and aggressive interactions.

*T*he Red-headed Woodpecker (9 inches long) is our only woodpecker with an all-red head and a body boldly patterned with large areas of black and white. Sexes look alike. Once a very common bird of the East, the Red-headed Woodpecker is now rather uncommon, though it is conspicuous due to its bright coloration, harsh calls, and tendency to occur in small colonies. It prefers open woods, groves, and orchards.

Queer Call (both sexes): A common call of the Red-headed Woodpecker is a loud, nasal *queer*. This call is similar to the Red-belly's *querr*, but is pitched higher and delivered more sharply. It probably functions as a contact call, but is given in a variety of situations when birds are aroused.

Drumming (both sexes): The drumming of the Red-head is rapid, has an even tempo, and often seems brief and weak in comparison with other woodpecker drums. Functions include territory advertisement, mate attraction, and pair maintenance.

Harsh *Churr* (both sexes): A sequence of harsh *churr*s is sometimes given during social interactions, especially when a bird takes flight. *Churr*s probably indicate a high state of arousal.

Rattle Call (both sexes): Red-headed Woodpeckers produce distinctive harsh rattles in a variety of situations. Rattles are given by solitary birds, by birds involved in social encounters, and by birds approaching their roost-hole at dusk.

The Northern Flicker (12 inches long) is an active, easily observed woodpecker found in residential areas across most of North America. The flicker has a brown, barred back, spotted underside, a black crescent bib, and a white rump that is noticeable in flight. Both sexes have a red spot on the nape; the male has a black mustache. Unlike other woodpeckers, flickers are often seen on lawns, where they search for insects, especially ants.

***Ki-ki-ki-ki* Call (both sexes):** Flickers of both sexes produce a loud sequence of rapidly repeated notes that can be heard from a considerable distance: *ki-ki-ki-ki-ki-ki* . . . This call lasts from about two to ten seconds (or longer) and probably has a variety of functions, including territory advertisement, mate attraction, and strengthening of the pair bond.

***Peough!* Call (both sexes):** A very distinctive flicker call is a sudden, down-slurred *peough!* This is thought to be a general contact call used by mates or members of a family group.

***Flicka-flicka* and *Eek-eek* calls (both sexes):** Flickers have two intimate encounter calls. One is a repeated *flicka-flicka-flicka* . . . with the accent on the first syllable of each phrase. The other is a drawn-out *eek-eek-eek* . . . Both calls occur during aggressive and courtship encounters, and they are often accompanied by pointing the bill upward and bobbing the head. Soft *flicka* calls are often given when mates interact near the nest.

Drumming (both sexes): The drum of the flicker has an even tempo and lasts a little over one second. Functions include mate attraction, territory advertisement, and maintenance of the pair bond.

*T*he Eastern Phoebe (7 inches long) is a member of the flycatcher family. Individuals of both sexes are dark brownish-gray above and pale below. They can be identified by their habit of bobbing their tails when perched. Phoebes frequent residential areas throughout eastern and central North America. They prefer wooded areas near water, where they feed on insects, spiders, ticks, and even small fish. Phoebes are migratory over the northern two-thirds of their range.

Song (males only): The male has two slightly different songs that it sings in rough alternation. Both song types sound something like the phrase *fee-bee*, but one has a buzzy ending and the other has a sputtery ending. The songs of all males sound very much alike.

***Zeek'-it* Call (both sexes):** As pairs move about during the courtship phase, the male often makes a short and emphatic *zeek'-it* just before landing on a perch. The female rarely utters this call as a greeting display.

Chatter Call (males only): A loud burst of harsh notes is given by males during the courtship phase. This chatter call is part of the male's nest-site-showing display, in which he shows a potential nest site to his mate by fluttering in front of the site and vocalizing.

***Chip* Call (both sexes):** High-pitched *chip*s are produced by phoebes in a variety of situations. Loud, repeated *chip*s are given in response to predators, especially near the nest. Males patrolling their territories periodically *chip* upon landing, and members of a pair or family group often use this note as a contact call.

Our largest American swallow, the Purple Martin (8 inches long) is a popular bird because of its colonial nesting habits and its attraction to "martin houses." Males are blue-black above and below. Females are light-bellied. Purple Martins prefer semi-open country and are often found near water. They have rich and melodious calls. Martins may gather by the thousands in late summer, prior to their migration to South America for the winter.

Cheur! Calls (both sexes): The common, all-purpose flocking or contact call of the martin is an emphatic *cheur!* that may be repeated excitedly. It occurs in a variety of situations during the breeding season and is the main call given by migrating birds.

Zee-zeert or Zeert Call (both sexes): In situations of alarm, martins utter loud, buzzy *zee-zeerts* or *zeerts*. Colonies erupt with these calls when a predator approaches.

Typical Song (males only): While perched near their nest, males sing short songs that are probably an expression of nest-site territoriality. Song usually begins with *cheur!* calls, then turns into a delightful warble, and finally ends with a loud terminal note.

Dawn Song (males only): During the hour or two before dawn, males sing a special dawn song that they give from a perch or while flying in the still-dark sky. Dawn songs are made up of repeated phrases of several types that sound quite unlike the other calls made by males. Each male has a distinctive set of phrases. It is possible that dawn song is used to attract unmated birds to the colony.

Chortle Calls (females only?): When perched near their nest, females express aggression toward neighboring females with soft, garbled chortle calls. Males are known to make a similar sound.

*I*ntroduced from Europe in the late 1800s, the European Starling (8 inches long) is now abundant throughout the continent, especially where humans are concentrated. The sexes look alike. In spring, starlings are iridescent-black and their bills are yellow. In winter, they are speckled and have black bills. Starlings are aggressive hole nesters that compete with native species for nesting sites. In the winter, they join other blackbirds to form huge flocks.

Typical Sounds (primarily males): Starlings are noisy during all seasons of the year, especially in the spring when groups gather in treetops. Common sounds include wheezy, whining, and wavering whistles, accompanied by an astounding variety of shrill squeaks, chatters, and chirps. One very distinctive sound is a steamy whistle that rises in pitch at the beginning, a version of which reminds many of a human "wolf whistle": *whee-ew!*

Song (males only): From late winter until summer, males produce elaborate vocal sequences that are considered song. These include sputtery and wheezy sounds, as well as melodic phrases and high-pitched, shrill notes. Inserted in the song are excellent imitations of the sounds of other species. There is no clear transition from the general calling of flocking birds to actual song, but singing males tend to perch by themselves near their nest site.

Harsh Chatter and *Chew!* Call (both sexes?): Sudden outbursts of harsh notes are given during aggressive encounters. Such calls often accompany chases. Another call presumed to indicate aggression is an emphatic *chew!* repeated slowly.

Distress Whines (both sexes): When captured or in extreme danger, excited starlings make harsh, squealing whines that can be heard at a considerable distance. Tape recordings of this call have been used to discourage flocking in residential areas.

Juvenile *Djjjj* Call (both sexes): In late summer, flocking juveniles make high-pitched *djjjj* calls. These distinctive calls function as begging sounds right after fledging, as scolding calls during encounters between juveniles, and as flocking calls.

28. Warbling Vireo

More often heard than seen, the plain-colored Warbling Vireo (5 inches long) sings its hurried, warbled song from high in the treetops. Pale gray-green above with a whitish breast, its distinguishing features are a white eyebrow and a faint dark line through the eye. Warbling Vireos are common from coast to coast; some scientists believe that eastern and western forms represent two distinct species. A tree-top bird, the male sings his charming song all day long through the summer months.

Song (males only): From dawn to dusk and from spring into autumn, males repeat their hurried song of warbled notes from high in treetops. Some-times they sing from the nest. Memory phrases include the following, spoken quickly: *If I could see one, I would seize one, and would squeeze one, 'til it squirts!* and *Iggley, pigelly, wiggely, pig!* Most songs end with a rising inflection.

***Eeah* and *Vit* Calls (both sexes):** Warbling Vireos have two basic call types. One is a nasal *eeah* and the other is a ticklike *vit*. Both calls are given in a variety of circumstances and may grade into other related calls. *Eeah*s and similar calls are used in courtship, but are also given in response to predators. When highly agitated or alarmed, vireos give *vit* calls in a rapid series.

One of the most widespread and familiar sparrows in North America, the Song Sparrow (6 inches long) graces the landscape each spring with its melodious songs, which have been immortalized by its scientific name, *Melospiza melodia*. Song Sparrows are reddish-brown with heavy breast streaks converging into a conspicuous central spot. Sexes are alike in appearance. Habitat varies widely over range, but Song Sparrows prefer brushy thickets, marshy areas, hedgerows, and lush gardens.

Song (males only): The song of the male is a variable series of notes, some being musical and others buzzy or trill-like. Many songs begin with several bright notes, followed by a jumble of short notes and trills. Individuals have a vocabulary of many different phrases that they combine into about ten different song patterns. They repeat one song type for a minute or more before switching to another. The essence of Song Sparrow song is difficult to describe, but the general pattern, or gestalt, is easily learned.

Seeep **Call (both sexes):** The contact note of the species is a high-pitched *seeep*. This sweet note is often given as birds take flight and is frequently heard in the weeks prior to migration.

Chimp **and** *Tsip* **Calls (both sexes):** When agitated, Song Sparrows produce two different calls. One is a hollow and nasal *chimp* or *tschenk*. Another is a high-pitched, metallic *tsip*. Upset birds often give both calls, especially around the nest.

Zeeee! **Call (both sexes):** Fledglings make a variety of buzzy calls, including a loud *zeeee!* that may be a begging call. Adults make a similar call when threatening other individuals during aggressive encounters.

30. Chipping Sparrow

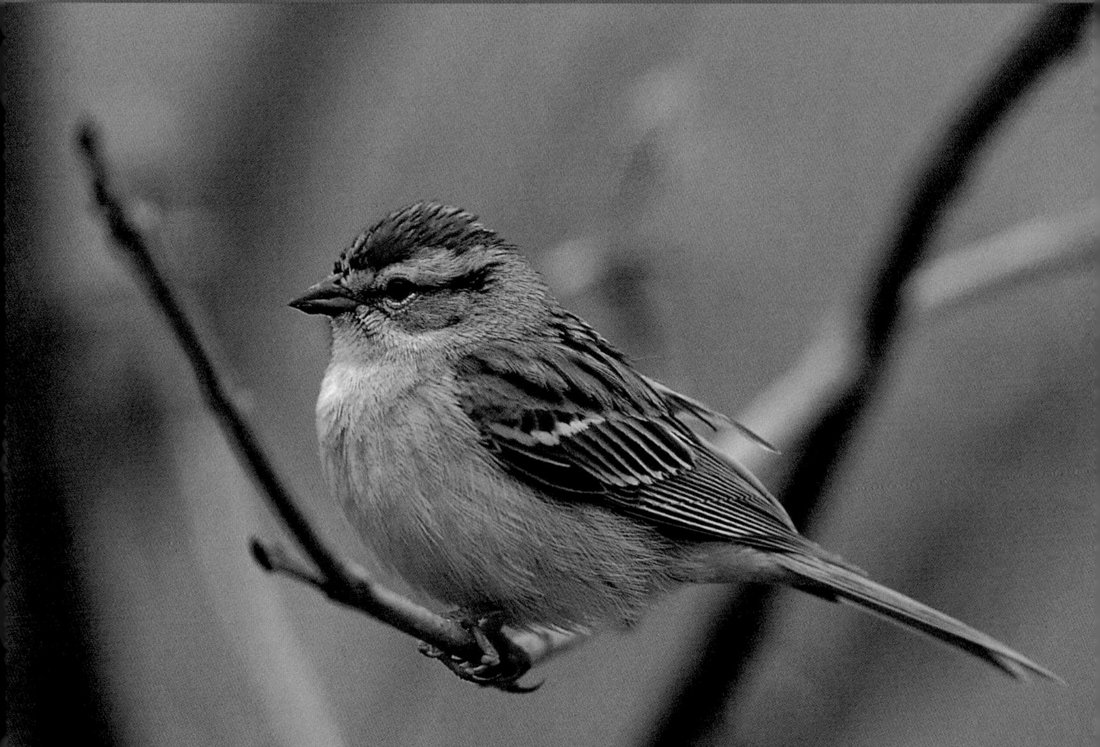

O ne of our most common backyard sparrows is the Chipping Sparrow (5 inches long), a species easily identified by its chestnut-brown cap and the broad white line above each eye. Chipping Sparrows are found throughout most of North America in habitats ranging from woodlands to open, grassy areas. They are migrants over most of their range. They nest in evergreens. Their cup-shaped nest of grass is lined with animal hair, usually black horsehair.

Song (males only): The trilled song of the male is a rapid series of dry *chip*s, lasting about two or three seconds. The *chip*s occur too rapidly to count and usually have a dull, unmusical quality. The songs of a given bird are all the same, although length may be varied. On the other hand, the trills of different birds vary considerably in quality, as does the rate of delivery of the *chip*s.

Tsk Call (both sexes): In a variety of alarm situations, especially around the nest, excited Chipping Sparrows make high-pitched *tsk* calls. *Tsk*s are also given at other times and may function as general contact notes.

Seeep Call and Quiet Twitter (both sexes?): During the courtship phase, pairs make high-pitched *seeep* calls as they move about together. When interacting, especially near the nest, they sometimes make quiet twitters made up of a rapid series of soft, high notes.

The Brown-headed Cowbird (7 inches long) is a small blackbird with a short, conical bill. The male is black with a coffee-brown head; the female is gray. Cowbirds are found in a variety of habitats across North America. The female does not build a nest. Instead, she lays her speckled white eggs in the nests of other bird species. Quite often, the noisy begging cowbird young is larger than the host bird trying to feed it!

Song (males only): Male song consists of several soft, bubbling notes followed by a loud, high-pitched squeak. Verbalizations of the song include *glub-glub-GLEEE* and *bub-lo-SEEE*. In the spring, singing males gather in treetops. When vocalizing, they ruff out their feathers, cock their wings, and tilt forward in a conspicuous manner. Females are usually perched nearby.

Chatter Call (females; rarely males): Female cowbirds make a chattering outburst of loud, liquid notes in a variety of situations. This sound may function as a contact call, but also seems to indicate aggression. Males sometimes make chatter calls.

Duetting (both sexes together): When pairs and larger groups perch together in treetops in the spring and early summer, females often give their chatter call just as the male sings. Such duetting may help develop and maintain pair bonds.

Whistle Call (males only): Upon taking flight, and during flight, males often give a loud whistle call composed of several high, squeaky notes. The first note is prolonged and is followed by one or more shorter notes: *seeeeesee*. This call may function as a contact note between mates. It is sometimes given by perched males.

***Chuck* Call (both sexes):** Soft, almost inaudible *chuck*s are often given by perched or feeding cowbirds. These may function as intimate contact calls. Louder versions possibly indicate alarm.

A common and conspicuous blackbird that frequents eastern and central residential areas is the Common Grackle (12 inches long). Grackles are large, irridescent black birds with bright yellow eyes and long, wedge-shaped tails. Females are smaller and duller than males. Grackles are gregarious and often nest in colonies in pines or cedars, where they can be heard making their raucuous squeaking calls.

***Chack* Call (both sexes):** The most common call of the grackle is a harsh *chack*, given by both sexes in diverse situations. It is often given in flight, and is the major call made by migrating birds.

Song (both sexes): The song of the grackle, given by both sexes, is a squeaky and harsh *squ-eek* or *scuda-leek*. Singing birds ruff out their feathers, cock their wings, and rise upward slightly. The entire display is referred to as a "ruff-out squeak." Migrating flocks do much singing, and individuals will give songs in flight. Female songs often terminate with *chaaa* calls.

***Chaaa* Call (females only):** A distinctive sound made by female grackles is a harsh, throaty *chaaa*. This call occurs during aggressive chases, and is often given when a female takes flight.

***Brrrt!* Call (males only):** Males periodically make a short, harsh, nasal call sounding something like *brrrt!* This call is given in a variety of circumstances and often induces nearby males to give the same call. Its exact function is not known.

An abundant and familiar bird of cities and villages is the House Sparrow (6 inches long), an Old World species introduced in Brooklyn in the mid-1800s and now a year-round resident in populated areas throughout most of North America. The male is recognized by his black throat, white cheeks, gray cap, and chestnut nape. The female is all brown, with an unstreaked breast. This noisy, gregarious species often builds its grassy, dome-shaped nest under eaves, among rafters, or behind shutters.

***Cheep* or *Cheeyup* Call-Series (both sexes):** During the breeding season, House Sparrows produce an extended series of loud and piercing *cheep* or *cheeyup* calls. Individuals usually give this call while perched near the nest, and a songlike function is generally assumed. Both sexes probably repeat the call to attract mates. Isolated *cheep*s may function as contact notes.

Nasal *T'whatit* (males only?): A distinctive House Sparrow call is a nasal *t'whatit, t'whatit*, made mostly by males. This call may communicate mild alarm, but its exact function is not known.

***Chu* or *Chu-chu* Calls (both sexes?):** When disturbed, individuals of both sexes produce an emphatic, nasal *chu* or *chu-chu*. These calls sometimes occur during social interactions.

Chatter Call (both sexes): During aggressive interactions, dominant individuals (usually males) make a harsh, drawn-out chatter. This call often accompanies chases and may be given as a House Sparrow attempts to drive away a predator.

***See-a-dee* Calls (both sexes?):** Another distinctive House Sparrow call is a high-pitched, shrill *see-a-dee*, which is repeated over and over. The function of this call is not clear.

The House Finch (5 1/2 inches long) is a western species introduced in the East in the 1940s. It is now a common year-round resident in most eastern urban and suburban areas. The male is brown with a bright red bib, a red band above his eye, and a red rump (in some populations, males are more orange than red). The female is all brown. Both sexes have streaked underparts. The House Finch is a sociable species that often visits feeders.

Song (males only): The pleasing song of the male is a bright, lively warble lasting several seconds and containing a variable mixture of musical notes and harsh phrases. Most songs contain one or more buzzy *zhree*es, and often terminate with an upwardly inflected *chur-wee*, a rapid *cherio*, or a nasal *che-urr*. Individual males commonly vary the length of their songs, and the songs of different males are often quite dissimilar.

Courtship Song (males only): When approaching a receptive female, courting males sing an excited and continuous version of song that includes an abundance of high, shrill notes. In response, the female crouches low and invites copulation.

***Chi-chuwee* Call (males only?):** A distinctive call, given primarily by males, sounds like *chi-chuwee*. This call may indicate mild arousal or alarm.

***Sweet!* or *Wheeet* Calls (both sexes):** A common call of the House Finch is a nasal *sweet!* or *wheeet*. This variable call is given throughout the year and functions primarily as a contact or flocking call. The *sweet!* is delivered sharply and emphatically, and sounds much like the House Sparrow's *cheep*. Winter flocks give a more nasal and drawn-out *wheeet*. The two extremes seem to intergrade one into the other.

35. Purple Finch

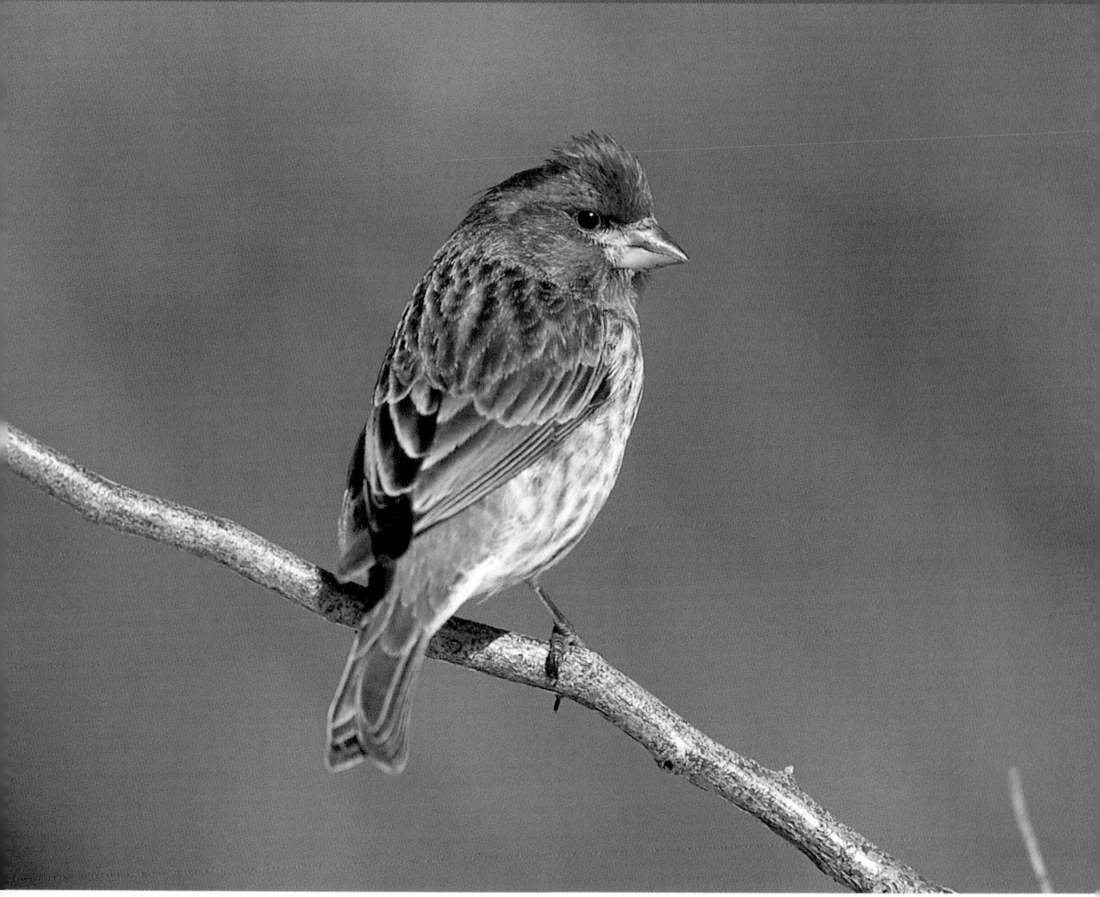

B reeding mostly in coniferous and mixed woods of the northern states, the male Purple Finch (6 inches long) is recognized by its raspberry red upperparts, breast, and sides. It lacks the streaking on the sides so typical of the House Finch. The female is brown above and heavily streaked below. The Purple Finch has a lively, warbled song that is sometimes extended into a long ramble. It often visits feeders but is far less common than the House Finch.

Song (males only): The variable song of the Purple Finch is a lively warble containing a mixture of harsh, buzzy phrases and musical utterances. It is easily confused with the House Finch's similar song. In the spring, males often sing together in small groups. Individuals may sing short songs sounding like a rapid warble, or extended, almost continuous songs containing bright, melodic passages. Songs are sometimes given in flight.

***Pit* Call (both sexes):** A common call of the Purple Finch is a dull *pit*. This sound probably functions as a contact call, but it may also indicate mild alarm. *Pit* calls are often given in flight.

Vireo Song (both sexes?): When individuals are highly agitated, they respond with a songlike alternation of distinctive phrases that remind many of the songpattern of a vireo. "Vireo song," as it is called, is produced during or after territorial encounters and may also be given in response to the presence of predators.

Master List of CD Contents

Species numbers are equivalent to track numbers on the compact disc. Each species is identified by name and number on the compact disc before its sound repertoire is presented. Written descriptions of each bird's repertoire can be located with ease within this book by referring to the appropriate species numbers as listed below or as heard on the disc.

1. **American Robin**
   Typical song
   Continuous song
   Peek and *tut* calls
   Whinny call
   High *seeee*
   Zeeeup!

2. **Northern Cardinal**
   Song
   Chip calls with volleys
   Chuck or *kwut* call
   Chip-kwut, chip-kwut
   Various calls during interaction

3. **Baltimore Oriole**
   Song
   Whistle calls
   Gee-gee-gee-gee and rapid chatter
   Fledgling *dee-dee-dee-dee*

4. **Orchard Oriole**
   Song
   Chatter call
   Chuck, chuck-seet! and whistle

5. **Tufted Titmouse**
   Typical songs
   Jway-jway
   Tsickajwee-jwee and *tseep*
   High *seeee* call-series

6. **Black-capped Chickadee**
   Song (*feee-bee-ee*)
   Chicka-dee-dee and *tseet* calls
   Gargle calls (*tseedleedeet*, etc.)
   High chatter
   High *see* call-series

7. **Carolina Chickadee**
   Four-note song (*fee-bee-fee-bay*)
   Five-note song
   Chicka-dee-dee
   Seep and raspy gargle calls
   Harsh chatter
   High *see* call-series

8. **White-breasted Nuthatch**
   Yank and *yank-yank*
   Excited *yank*-series
   Ik calls
   Song (*hey-hey-hey-hey-hey*)
   Whining calls, including *pheeoo*

9. **House Wren**
   Song
   Shrill song
   *Chit*s, *churr*s, and *churr-chit*s
   Rattle calls
   Buzz calls

10. **Carolina Wren**
    Song
    Male *cheer* and female *dit-dit*
    Male *pink* or *p'dink*
    Female chatter
    Raspy *churr* call

11. Cedar Waxwing
Hissy *seeee* calls
Buzzy trills (*bzeee*)
Excited trills (food-begging)

12. Gray Catbird
Song with *mew* calls
Mew call
Kwut calls
Ratchet call

13. Brown Thrasher
Song
Smack! call
Burry *teeeoo*
Harsh *chjjj*

14. Northern Mockingbird
Song with mimicry
Chewk call
Harsh *chjjj*
Chitichick! with *chjjj* calls

15. Blue Jay
Jay and *jay-jay* calls
Tool-ool, tweedlee, etc.
Comb call
Kew calls and subtle whines
Hawk imitation

16. American Crow
Caw! and variants
Mobbing calls
Juvenile nasal calls and growls
Rattle call
Too-doo and *crrracko*

17. Chimney Swift
Chitter call
Group chittering
Chip call-series (trio flight)

18. Rock Dove
Display coo
Perch coo (moaning)
Wing-clapping and whirring

19. Mourning Dove
Long coo
Short coo
Wing twitter

20. Eastern Screech-Owl
Whinny call
Monotonic trill
Juvenile trill
Alarm whines and bill-snaps

21. Ruby-throated Hummingbird
Squeaky *chip*s and wing hum
Chase call
Wing-boxing and *tseep* call
Pendulum arc buzz

22. Red-bellied Woodpecker
Querr call and drumming
Chi calls and chatter-*chi*
Harsh *churr*
Woika-woika-woika and other calls

23. Red-headed Woodpecker
Queer call
Drumming
Harsh *churr*
Rattle call

24. Northern Flicker
Ki-ki-ki-ki call
Peough call
Flicka-flicka and *eek-eek*
Drumming

25. Eastern Phoebe
Song
Zeek'-it call
Chatter call
Chip call

26. Purple Martin
Cheur! call
Zee-zeert and *zeert*
Typical song
Dawn song
Chortle calls

27. European Starling
Typical sounds
Song with mimicry
Harsh chatter and *chew!*
Distress whine
Juvenile *djjjj* call

28. Warbling Vireo
Song
Eeeah and *vit* calls

29. Song Sparrow
Song
Seeep call
Chimp and *tsip* calls
Buzzy *zeeee!* call

30. Chipping Sparrow
Song
Tsk call
Seeep call and quiet twitter

31. Brown-headed Cowbird
Song
Chatter call
Whistle call
Chuck call

32. Common Grackle
Chack call
Song
Chaaa call
Brrrt! call

33. House Sparrow
Cheep or *cheeyup* call-series
T'whatit call
Chu or *chu-chu* call
Chatter call
See-a-dee call

34. House Finch
Typical song
Courtship song
Chi-chuwee call
Sweet! and *wheeet* calls

35. Purple Finch
Song
Group singing
Pit call
Vireo song